DESERT FOOTHILLS LIBRARY

T 48758

D0601950

J
942
LIS
Lister, Maree
Welcome to England.

DESERT FOOTHILLS LIBRARY
P.O. BOX 4070
CAVE CREEK, AZ 85327
488-2286

GAYLORD FG

SEP 17 1999

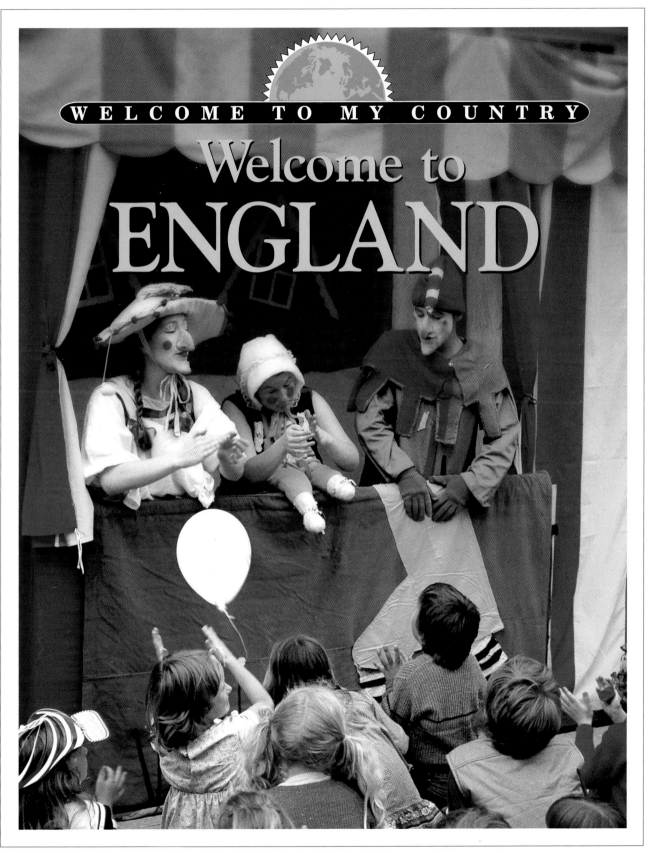

WELCOME TO MY COUNTRY

Welcome to
ENGLAND

Gareth Stevens Publishing
MILWAUKEE

DESERT FOOTHILLS LIBRARY
P.O. BOX 4070
CAVE CREEK, AZ 85327

Written by
MAREE LISTER and **MARTI SEVIER/**
ROSELINE NGCHEONG-LUM

Designed by
LYNN CHIN NYUK LING

Picture research by
SUSAN JANE MANUEL

First published in North America in 1999 by
Gareth Stevens Publishing
1555 North RiverCenter Drive, Suite 201
Milwaukee, Wisconsin 53212 USA

For a free color catalog describing
Gareth Stevens Publishing's list of high-quality books
and multimedia programs, call
1-800-542-2595 (USA) or
1-800-461-9120 (CANADA).
Gareth Stevens Publishing's
Fax: (414) 225-0377

All rights reserved. No part of this book may be reproduced or
utilized in any form or by any means electronic or mechanical,
including photocopying, recording, or by an information storage and
retrieval system, without permission from the copyright owner.

© **TIMES EDITIONS PTE LTD 1999**
Originated and designed by
Times Books International
an imprint of Times Editions Pte Ltd
Times Centre, 1 New Industrial Road
Singapore 536196
http://www.timesone.com.sg/te

Library of Congress Cataloging-in-Publication Data

Lister, Maree.
Welcome to England / Maree Lister, Marti Sevier, and
Roseline NgCheong-Lum.
p. cm. — (Welcome to my country)
Includes bibliographical references and index.
Summary: An overview of the country of England that includes
information on geography, history, government, the economy,
people, and lifestyles.
ISBN 0-8368-2396-6 (lib. bdg.)
1. England—Juvenile literature. [1. England.]
I. Sevier, Marti. II. NgCheong-Lum, Roseline, 1962-
III. Title. IV. Series.
DA27.5.L58 1999
942—dc21 99-14248

Printed in Malaysia

1 2 3 4 5 6 7 8 9 03 02 01 00 99

PICTURE CREDITS
A.N.A. Press Agency: 36, 45
Andes Press Agency: 9 (bottom), 31, 38
Axiom: 6, 39 (top)
Bes Stock: 2, 8, 22
Sylvia Cordaiy Photo Library: cover, 3 (top),
    4, 26, 27, 37
Ron Emmons: 29 (top)
Hutchison Library: 1, 3 (bottom), 30, 35
Illustrated London News Picture Library:
    13, 14, 29 (bottom), 33
International Photobank: 5, 7, 11
Life File: 20, 23
Christine Osborne: 40
Photobank Photolibrary: 16, 17, 21
Liba Taylor: 10
Topham Picturepoint: 3 (center), 9 (top), 12,
    15 (all), 18, 28, 32, 34, 39 (bottom)
Travel Ink: 19, 24, 25, 41

Digital Scanning by Superskill Graphics Pte Ltd

Contents

Words that appear in the glossary are printed in **boldface** type the first time they occur in the text.

Welcome to England!

England has been a world leader for hundreds of years. The English people have **invented** many things and traveled to many places. England, Scotland, Wales, and Northern Ireland make up the United Kingdom. Come visit England and the English people.

Opposite: Trafalgar Square in London is home to many friendly pigeons.

Below: The numerous fishing villages in England are very popular with artists.

The Flag of England

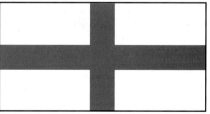

The flag of England has a red cross on a white background. It is called the cross of St. George, the patron saint of England. The Union Jack is the flag of the United Kingdom.

The Land

England is a small country, making up about half of the area of the United Kingdom. With a land area of 50,000 square miles (129,500 square kilometers), it is about the size of the state of Louisiana. Its neighbors are Scotland to the north, and Wales to the east. The southwestern tip of the country is called Land's End.

Below: A farmhouse is nestled at the foot of a mountain in the Cumbrian region.

England is mostly flat, with a few mountains in the north. At 3,210 feet (978 meters) in height, the tallest mountain is Scafell Pike. It is located in a region called the Lake District. This region is also home to England's largest lake, Lake Windermere. The longest river is the River Thames. It starts in the Cotswold Hills in the west country and cuts across southern England to London.

Above: Mevagissey is a village in Cornwall near Land's End.

Seasons

The English climate is mild. Winters are cold but not freezing, and summers are not very hot. However, the country receives substantial rainfall. It rains in some areas all year, with the wettest weather in the Lake District. In winter, the coast is battered by strong winds called gales.

Left: Bright yellow daffodils announce the beginning of the spring season.

Plants and Animals

Green **pastures** cover most of the countryside in England. Although there are not very many forests, parks and gardens fill with colorful flowers in spring.

The largest English animal is the red deer. Other animals prowling the countryside include foxes, badgers, stoats, and voles. Many species of birds can be spotted in the English skies and fish in the rivers and seas. Seals live in the shallow waters off the east coast of England.

Top: In England, foxes threaten farm animals, so some farmers hunt them. Many people think foxes should be protected from being hunted.

Bottom: The rose is England's national flower.

History

The earliest known people living in England were the **Celts** who came from central Europe. In 55 B.C., the Roman emperor Julius Caesar defeated the Celts and made England part of the **Roman Empire**. Although the local tribes rebelled time and again, the Romans ruled England for nearly five hundred years. They brought Christianity to the Celts, and various improvements to daily life.

Below: During the time of the Roman Empire, these hot spring baths were used for medicinal purposes. The Romans named the town *Aquae Sulis*, or Bath.

Left: King Arthur's round table hangs on a wall of Winchester Cathedral. Arthur was a legendary king who gathered a collection of knights to fight evil.

In A.D. 406, the Romans were called back to Rome. By A.D. 600, German people, known as Anglo-Saxons, ruled England. In 1066, William the Conqueror from France became king. During the **Middle Ages** (1100–1400), England took part in the **Crusades**, an attempt by Christians to take back Jerusalem from the Muslims.

Change and Expansion

In 1534, King Henry VIII set up the **Church of England**, or Anglican Church. As head of the new Church, he replaced the Catholic pope as religious leader of England. After Henry's death, Catholics and Anglicans fought for control over England. These struggles took place during the Reformation, a long period of change within Christianity.

Henry's daughter, Queen Elizabeth I, helped expand England in the second half of the sixteenth century. During her reign, English explorers colonized many parts of Africa, Asia, and America. The **colonies** provided great wealth for England. However, the American colonies were not happy under English rule. They proclaimed independence in 1776 and defeated the English after seven years of fighting. American independence was granted in 1783.

Above: The Duke of Wellington won many battles for England in the eighteenth century.

Opposite: Queen Elizabeth I ruled England for forty-five years. She made the Anglican Church England's main religious body.

Left: During both World Wars, women worked while men defended the country. Many women worked in factories that produced weapons and medicines.

The Twentieth Century

England suffered great losses during the two World Wars. Soldiers died fighting, and major cities were bombed. After World War II, colonies such as India and Burma (Myanmar) became independent. England's economy recovered after the wars. Today, England is a major partner in the **European Union** (EU) and is a strong influence on world politics.

King Henry VIII (1491–1547)

Henry VIII is famous for his six wives. His first wife could not give him a son, so he wanted to remarry. The Catholic Church did not allow this, so he created the Church of England and divorced his wife.

Henry VIII

William Shakespeare (1564–1616)

William Shakespeare wrote many poems and plays that have been translated into many languages. Most high school students in English-speaking countries study some of Shakespeare's plays.

William Shakespeare

Margaret Thatcher (1925–)

Margaret Thatcher became the first woman prime minister of England in 1979. She was called the "Iron Lady" because of her strong views and forceful manner.

Margaret Thatcher

Government and the Economy

Government

The English style of government is called a **parliamentary monarchy**. This means that the country is governed by an elected parliament, with its king or queen as a **symbolic** head. Although Queen Elizabeth II is the ruler of the country, she has no power to make decisions on her own.

Below: The Trooping of the Colour is a grand pageant during the Queen's birthday celebration.

The power to make decisions rests with the parliament, made up of the House of Lords and the House of Commons. Only members of the House of Commons are elected by the people. They are called members of parliament, or MPs. The head of government is the prime minister, the leader of the party in power. The two dominant parties are the Conservatives and Labour.

Above: The Houses of Parliament are at Westminster on the bank of the River Thames in London. To the right is the famous clock tower, **Big Ben**.

Economy

England is one of the richest countries in the world. Although it does not have many natural resources, the country is very advanced in industry and finance. England is the largest producer of aircraft in Western Europe and **exports** many of its goods to the rest of the world. Its two biggest trading partners are Germany and the United States.

Above: Great Britain has its own supply of oil in the North Sea.

Agriculture is still an important part of the economy in England. Although very few people work in agriculture, English farms supply two-thirds of the country's needs thanks to modern farm machinery. The most important crops are barley and wheat. Potatoes, the staple food, are grown in large quantities. Dairy farming is important in England, too. Cows and sheep produce top-quality meats, milk, and cheeses.

Below: Dairy farming is most common in areas where there is heavy rainfall.

People and Lifestyle

People

The English population is a mixture of cultures, with **immigrants** arriving from all over the world. Ninety-six

Left: Many people from former English colonies, such as the West Indies, have settled in England. Immigrants also come from various parts of Europe.

percent of the population is fair-skinned. **Minorities** form about 4 percent of the population, with Asians making up the largest group, followed by West Indians and Africans.

The English people are still very conscious about **social classes**. People from different classes do not often mix.

Above: Some young people sport colorful hairstyles and wear black leather and chains. Many hold regular jobs and dress in this "punk" style in their free time.

Left: This upper-class families likes to meet for tea in the garden.

Family Life

English families tend to be small, with two or three children. Many couples are not married but live together. Single-parent families are also becoming more common. Grandparents play an important role in child care, especially for single-parent families.

Many English women choose to continue their careers after having children. Most of them do so because they have families to support. Others work because they enjoy their careers.

Teenage pregnancy is a growing problem in England. Many young girls have to abandon their education to care for the children.

Below: Despite receiving unemployment benefits, many young people in England are homeless.

Education

Almost everybody in England can read and write. English children must go to school from age five to sixteen. When they are sixteen, students take an examination to decide if they should continue with school or take a job. Most of them leave school after this exam. Only one-quarter of the students continue their schooling for two more years and then enroll in a university to earn a **degree**.

Below: Young children get help from older brothers and sisters with their homework.

English children enjoy many activities at school. Sports are very popular. Boys play **soccer**, hockey, and rugby, which is similar to football. Girls enjoy hockey, netball, and gymnastics. Students also go on trips to see historical buildings, and even across the channel to France, where they practice their French.

Above: Graduation day is a good opportunity to take pictures with family and friends.

Religion

In England, people are free to choose their religion. Children receive religious education at school.

Nearly half of the English population belongs to the Church

Below: St. Paul's Cathedral is the most famous Anglican church in England.

Below: St. Paul's Cathedral is the most famous Anglican church in England.

of England. Others belong to a different Christian denomination or have no religion at all. Most Asians are Muslims.

The most important religious festival in England is Christmas. Even non-Christians take part in the festivities. People attend church services and sing carols. They eat roast turkey and Christmas pudding,

a traditional cake made with dried fruit and liquor. Many homes have a Christmas tree with pretty decorations and colorful lights.

Above: The entire family gathers for Christmas dinner. At Christmastime, people exchange cards and gifts.

Language

The English spoken in England today comes from Anglo-Saxon, a German dialect. It also contains many words taken from Latin and French.

Left: Geoffrey Chaucer (1342/43–1400) was one of the first writers in the English language. He wrote *The Canterbury Tales*.

Left: English spelling was not finalized until the eighteenth century. This gravestone from the seventeenth century shows how words were spelled differently than they are today.

Literature

The first story in the English language was that of Beowulf, a brave hero. English literature deals with many issues — love, adventure, fantasy, and social justice.

English women started writing books in the eighteenth century. At first, the authors used male names to hide the fact that they were women. Today, the most famous children's writer is Enid Blyton, whose adventure stories are read by thousands of children.

Below: In his novels, Charles Dickens wrote about the suffering of poor people in nineteenth-century England.

Arts

The Celts made beautiful jewelry and clothing from metals and precious stones. Warriors wore helmets and carried swords studded with gems.

Left: The art of stained glass was very popular in England in the Middle Ages.

Later, English artists turned to sculpture and carving. They made beautiful statues in stone, and carved objects in wood, ivory, and bone. They also turned their attention to decorating houses with embroidered rugs and mats. Another important art form was the writing of script. Before the printing press was invented, books were written by hand and decorated with illustrations.

Above: In London's **West End**, theaters abound. Theater is one of England's most respected and accomplished art forms.

Modern Art

The two most well-known English painters are John Constable and Joseph Turner. They both lived during the nineteenth century. Constable painted many scenes of the English countryside. Turner was famous for his landscapes and seascapes in watercolor.

Below: Adorning the grounds of a building is a piece of modern art by English sculptor Henry Moore.

Music

At the beginning of the twentieth century, Edward Elgar composed classical music, while the team of Gilbert and Sullivan put on lively musicals. The most famous modern composer of musicals is Andrew Lloyd Weber. In the 1960s, English bands the Beatles and the Rolling Stones became popular worldwide.

Above: In the early 1900s, the work of English composer Edward Elgar reflected England's prosperity.

Films

The English film industry has produced many magnificent movies. The first English movie star was Charlie Chaplin, a genius in filmmaking. A well-known English film hero is James Bond, who has been thrilling moviegoers for more than twenty years.

The **British Broadcasting Corporation** (BBC) produces excellent radio programs and television documentaries.

Leisure

Many English people spend a lot of time in their gardens, planting and **pruning**. They are very proud of their colorful flowers and green lawns.

Left: Punch and Judy shows began in the 1600s. They are still very popular with children.

Children like to read and watch television. When the weather is dry, they like to play in the garden. One interesting game is called "conkers." Players tie a nut called a horse chestnut to a string and try to break their friend's chestnut with it.

English families enjoy long walks in the countryside or along the rugged coastlines of England. Hunting and fishing are other popular hobbies.

Above: Many children watch television when they come home from school and on weekends.

Sports

England is a nation of sports-lovers. The English invented many of the sports played today. All students participate in sports, and the country produces world-class athletes.

The most popular sport in England is soccer. Boys compete with each other on school teams. Some girls play soccer, too. Professional soccer games attract large crowds on weekends.

Above: Rowing is a popular university sport. The most famous rowing event in England is between Oxford and Cambridge universities.

Rugby is a sport played by most schoolboys. There are fifteen players to a team, and the object of the game is to score points by touching the ball over the end line. Rugby is similar to American football.

Below: Rugby season runs from September to April. Various tournaments are played.

One sport in which England excels worldwide is hockey. Both the men's and women's hockey teams often win medals at the Olympics and at other international competitions.

Festivals

Many English festivals date from pre-Christian times. May Day is still celebrated as the first day of spring. Young girls dance around a **maypole**, and Morris dancers perform folk dances in the streets.

Halloween began as a Celtic feast called Samhain. The Celts believed that the dead returned to life on that night. People lit bonfires to keep evil

Below: Folk dancers known as Morris dancers perform on various occasions. They carry sticks and wear bells around their ankles.

Left: Started by the West Indian community in England, the Notting Hill Carnival draws crowds and participants from all over the world.

Below: Guy Fawkes night celebrates a failed attempt to blow up parliament in 1605. People light bonfires and set off fireworks to mark the occasion.

spirits away, and children played mischievous tricks. This was the origin of today's trick-or-treating.

Easter begins with Shrove Tuesday, or "Pancake Day." Then comes Lent, traditionally a forty-day period of fasting. Today, some people give up favorite foods or bad habits. On Easter Day itself, children search for chocolate eggs in their gardens.

Food

Potatoes are eaten at most meals in England, together with meat and fresh vegetables. Fish and chips is a traditional English fast food. Chinese food, Indian curries, and Middle Eastern kebabs are becoming popular.

Above: Traditional fish and chips is wrapped in newspaper and served with salt and vinegar.

Opposite: Children usually have lunch at school. This meal used to be high in fat, but schools are changing to healthier foods.

Sunday Lunch

Most families get together for Sunday lunch. A typical Sunday lunch would be roast beef, Yorkshire pudding (a type of pancake), roast potatoes, and vegetables. Some families meet at their local pub for lunch.

Funny Names

Some dishes have funny names. "Spotted dick" is a steamed pudding made with raisins, flour, and eggs. Children also love "toad-in-the-hole," which is a dish of sausages baked in a tasty batter.

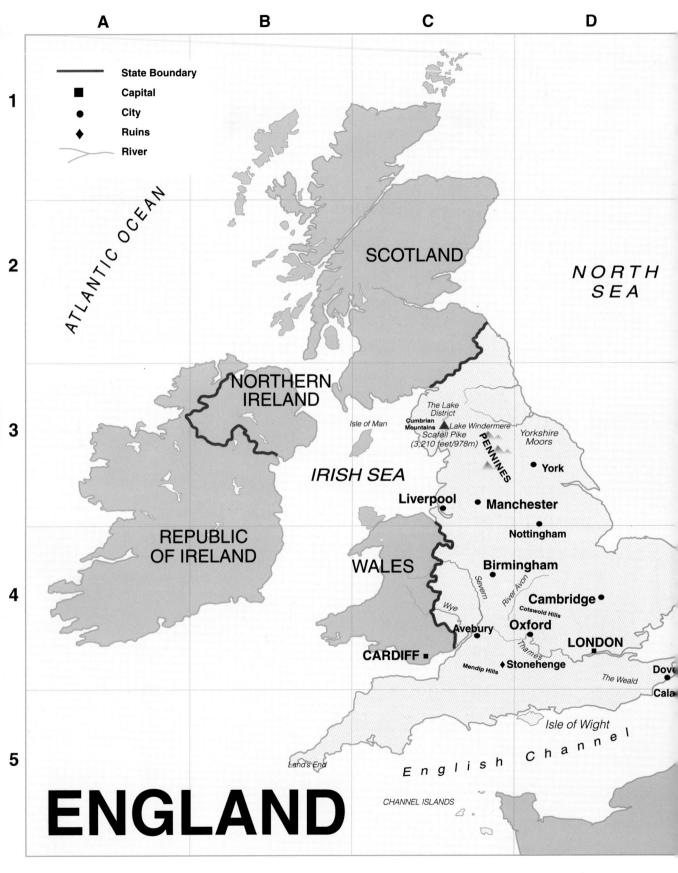

A   B   C   D

1

State Boundary
■ Capital
● City
◆ Ruins
River

2

ATLANTIC OCEAN

SCOTLAND

NORTH SEA

3

NORTHERN
IRELAND

Isle of Man

The Lake District
Cumbrian Mountains
Scafell Pike
(3,210 feet/978m) ▲ Lake Windermere

Yorkshire Moors

PENNINES

● York

IRISH SEA

REPUBLIC
OF IRELAND

Liverpool ●

● **Manchester**

● Nottingham

WALES

Birmingham

Severn

River Avon

Cambridge ●

Cotswold Hills

4

Wye

Avebury ●

Oxford

Thames

LONDON ■

CARDIFF ■

Mendip Hills

◆ **Stonehenge**

The Weald

Dove●

Cala●

Isle of Wight

5

English Channel

Land's End

CHANNEL ISLANDS

ENGLAND

42

E

NORWAY

N

THE
ETHERLANDS

BELGIUM

FRANCE

Above: The rocky coastline of Cornwall.

Quick Facts

Official Name	England (part of the United Kingdom)
Capital	London
Official Language	English
Population	47,500,000
Land Area	50,000 square miles (129,500 sq. km)
Highest Point	Scafell Pike (3,210 feet/978 m)
Major Rivers	Avon, Thames, Trent
Main Religion	Church of England (often called Anglican)
Major Festivals	May Day, May 1
	Halloween, October 31
	Christmas, December 25
Major Cities	Birmingham, Leeds, Liverpool, Manchester, Sheffield
Head of State	The monarch (Queen Elizabeth II as of 1952; however, the country is ruled by parliament)
National Anthem	"God Save the Queen"
National Flag	Cross of St. George
Currency	Pound Sterling (£ 0.61 = U.S. $1 in 1999)

Opposite: Rescue services patrol national parks to ensure the safety of hikers.

Index